heavy with water
and music

sarah mykel samuel

CONTENTS

PROLOGUE

I thought I heard music
But it was just my pee, sprinkling
The surface of the water
In the toilet bowl

RAISE YOUR HAND BEFORE SPEAKING

I always liked to follow the rules:
Raise your hand before speaking
Sit in your chair until the bell rings
Don't tell your best friend's boyfriend that you love him

I like to look up words in the dictionary:
Friendship
Morality
Betrayal
Love

I still don't know what they mean, exactly
But I know how to keep to myself
Like dry ink in a diary
Or wet gum under a pew

I have never been taught
How to live a good life,
One of dignity
And courage
And rage
By which I mean, fire

But I have learned to say to myself
Over and over and over again:

Never be afraid that you don't fit in
That who you are is bad or evil or wrong
You were made for this world
Let it see you
You are not a rough draft or an outcast or an extra
You are an artist

CHAPTER ONE

I like my coffee black
With cream and sugar on the side
In a pastry

BREAKING THE RULES

When I walked home tonight
at two in the morning

it had been snowing lightly
for a couple of hours

and the sidewalks
were indistinguishable
from the streets

                                higher
                         bit
                   little
except that they were a
but everything was white
so I walked in the middle
of the road and made

          d
           e
          s
            i
          g
          n
            s

with my
footprints

FOUR MINUTES ON THE 10th FLOOR OF BOBST

Have you noticed the increase in security? He said.
I had and I asked why.
Suicide attempt, he said.
I thought it might be.

He didn't ask her name
Or if she likes to eat her lettuce plain.
He didn't think I'd know.

10:45pm-3:00am

shot
beer

shot
beer

beer

shot

shot

taco
taco

sleep

MAYBE IT'S THE WINE

I cried at the bar again last night.
People saw
my melting face
and asked me what was wrong
and I told them
I didn't know,
The only thing I can think is I'm

so

impossibly

lonely

Or maybe it's the wine.

PSYCHOSIS

In this song, he said
she's singing about my empire

Your empire?

I was blessed with an empire, he said
You know how the stars resemble someone?
Well, it's me

That's funny, I said
I always thought they kind of resembled me...

QUICKSAND

I am coming up
out of the mud, out of the sludge
where heavy souls go to rest
and feel like failures,
where all our fears are loud and
ringing in our bones.

I am walking into Hell and saying "Hello,
thank you for having me.
The tapestries are lovely."

I have never fallen into quicksand,
but I expect it's something like that day in Maine
when the beach was pretty and I couldn't see it
when the rocks and shells were perfectly in place,
telling stories of how we are all connected,
how beauty hides in everything
and all you have to do is notice.

And I missed the whole thing,
covered in sweat and mosquito bites,
though all I could feel was gravity.
My soul had fallen into quicksand,
dragged to the bottom of loneliness.
I thought that I might drown
that day. I thought the ocean,
obviously made of tears
because my eyes were dry,
might come to the shore and
ask for me, and I would go
out into its empty
center, where I would have
nowhere to go and nothing to
hold onto, where I would get

18

tired of treading water,
of holding my breath,
where I would finally have to let go
and leave my body to the seaweed and the waves.

EXPLAIN WHY YOU WOULD NOT LIKE TO BE MARRIED SOMEDAY
4-30-99

Right now boys are grows and mean and I don't like them so I definitely don't want to get married. If I do get married I will not marry someone who smokes. If I find someone who I really like than I will get married but the chances are I'm not going to find someone. If I get married, the boy will have to be: Smart, funny, not drug taking of any kind unless he is sick, younger than me so I can boss him around, and fun to be with. I will not get married till I'm 26 if I do get married. I will have to know the boy for the least amount 2 years and I don't have a maximum of years.

PLACES I NEVER LIVED: DANI'S HOUSE

I never lived at Dani's house, but I might as well have. She was my best friend from 2nd through 5th grade. We were still good friends after that, but the titles get blurry. I went to her house almost every day after school and slept on the bottom part of her trundle bed as much as I slept in my own bed. Maybe that's why, even now, I prefer not to sleep alone. We always fell asleep to lullabies, which is something I never did at my own house. Either lullabies or me telling her over and over again about whichever boy I had a crush on until she finally asked me to be quiet.

Dani and I did everything together. We went to school together. We took baths together. We did plays together. We even wrote our own play together. I was at her house the day her cat got ran over by a car. She came to my grandma's funeral. But we didn't go to each other's birthday parties. Both of our birthdays are on holidays and we were always out of town with our families.

CHAPTER TWO

If you want to draw a mushroom,
draw a mushroom.

COAST TO COAST

Welcome me,
sunshine on the beach.
Kiss my *kepele*
Hello.
Help me forget stale memories,
molding and fuzzy and brown.
Build me a future out of sand
castles and Mexican food,
margaritas and driving with the top down.

Remember me, walking city,
breathing city.
Remember my footprints
in the snow,
my hot breath on your cold,
indifferent nights.
I snuck my soul into black coffee and
cherry blossom trees, rooftops and the cracks
in your gum-speckled sidewalks. Keep it for me.
I'll be back to dance on the tops of your very big feet.

A WISH TO CARRY DANDELION SEEDS

Last night, I cried .
A deep, drunken cry.
A thousand tears for the
way things are.
Lonely whiskey dinners
was not what I had wished for
on shooting stars and birthday candles.
I did not send coins down wishing wells
to deliver the request:

Let me feel alone forever.

I did not mean to poison my body
in search of love.

I did not mean to poison my body
just so I could say *I'm sorry*
I can't see my own perfection. I'm sorry
that I put you on a pedestal.

Maybe, instead of wishing on fallen
eyelashes for someone
to make me feel beautiful,
I should have wished for the strength to cry
in front of people. To cry without a reason
other than Surrender.
To cry and say

This isn't what I wanted

and to grieve.

THERE ARE RAINBOWS IN THE SPRINKLERS

I am tired of bored
and reluctant
Good Mornings
when the sun lights up a blue sky
and there are rainbows in the sprinklers.

I want to speak full words,
still pulsing with thought
still alive and ringing.
There are *rainbows in the sprinklers*, after all
and the flowers are so pretty.

NEW YEARS EVE

At the party there's a photo booth
and I like to watch you dancing to rap music
under the 40 watt chandelier light in the living room,
a beer in one hand and a bottle of whiskey in the other.

The champagne is in the kitchen, corks out,
with nothing left to wait for.
I'm not drinking, but I had half a glass at midnight
and the bubbles filled in holes
carved out from empty conversation,
until they popped.

I want to feel the mountains,
so gigantic and majestic,
but they're just dirt and trees and rocks
under my fingers, just dust under my feet,
and you're just like a hologram.

Six strangers insert my name into a happy birthday song
while you talk to your friend, and I realize
I have nothing left to offer but a memory of a good time,
an abstraction of love, and a plastic red cup
full of sparkling apple cider.

ADVICE FROM THE FLOOR OF MY BEDROOM

Try not to have too many fun experiences when you're young.

You'll just have to think about them and be sad later when you get older and nothing is going your way.

A PARKING SPOT AT NOON ON THURSDAY

I high fived a plant the other day, because its leaves
Were sticking out over the plaster wall above the sidewalk
Congratulating me for being so alive and breathing
And for a little while, I would wave
And the world waved back

A row of yellow flowers
A parking spot at noon on Thursday

And I knew that the ground would hold me by my shoes
Inviting my next step.

But what if the ground gets tired
Bruised and battered?

Another person asked me
What I did for work and I told them
My usual answer, that I didn't,
Making up excuses that make me sound
Too busy

And today as I stood looking out at the ocean
And the way people walk so clumsily but determined
In the sand
I realized that my life is my work
That the universe
In the way the water looks like music
The way the breeze moves unapologetically through my hair
As if we were alone
The way even the piping looks beautiful among the rocks
On the side of the cliff
And even you, my dear,
Are both my customers and my boss and most especially
My muse.

CANAL ST, NYC

Canal Street was never quite the same
Once you were on the ground
Eye level with traffic
And the smells of chicken
And trash
It was crowded from up close
And in the summer, quite hot and sticky
Nothing like you would imagine
From the fire escape three stories
Above
It was easy to imagine romance
The buses on circuit
Tourists waving
A bubble gun in your right hand
And the colors of soapy spheres
Above the city
Floating, as if beauty were just an easy fact
Of life
But it's the rooftops I remember most
At night, a little drunk
I could rarely see the stars
But the lights of the city
Were stars enough for me
There's nothing that can beat
The feeling that you belong in a place
And that it loves you

THOUGHTS IN A COFFEE SHOP

I keep having to remind myself that I'm not waiting for something
or going anywhere,
that I'm just sitting
in a coffee shop, reading poems
and watching people talk
and type out screenplays
while my tea cools.

I keep having to remind myself that this is life,
that it's already started, that I'm already in
the river.

And when I do remember that this right here,
this sound of clinking dishes and people
talking, this pen in my hand and my tea
getting cold, that this is it,
my body welcomes me
back into the empty moment and I can finally stop
rushing to the elusive holy grail of a purpose.
And I can sit back and say with pride:

Look at all I have created so far.

And for a moment, the question of whether
or not I have a place in this Universe
is not even a thought in my
grateful
and contented
mind.

FIRST DAY OF SPRING

I thought it would be a good idea
remembering that today is the first day
of spring, to write a poem
everyday
and compile it into a book
called "Spring".
I thought it would be romantic
and that the wide-eyed brightness
of the new season would shape
my words into a beautiful
declaration, an announcement
of my own rebirth into this world—

A new woman
A blossoming rose, as they say
A person who had finally found who she was
And what she had to give away.

But as it turns out,
I don't know how to write the world,
don't know what to make of it.
I only know how to watch it
from the inside and feel the way
my heart sometimes sends
signals to my fingertips
my feet
my face
and says *Touch that*
      Go there
      Cry a tear of grief or recognition

THE BIG LOVE

I don't know if the boy I like
Likes me back
Or not
And for the first time I can see
That it doesn't matter
That in fact he is not even real
Just a hologram or a mirror
Or an imaginary friend I made up
Out of loneliness and a desire
To know myself. That in fact, this time,
The grieving is for all the ways
I've refused to melt
Into the great big Love, the endless gap
So uncomfortable and frightening.

Though as it turns out, it is not even a gap after all,
But a door, inviting me infinitely
Into the next thing
Into the big love,
To the true home where I belong.

And now I sit, staring out the window,
slowly relinquishing my tight
And painful hold
Freedom is at the end of this
Though I don't know when I will experience
the delicious space within me.
To be friends with the gripping,
This is my task for now.

Suddenly
The only thing that's left of me
Is my last breath
The one I must exhale

—

Leaving everything I ever was behind
Ready, courageously, for the next
Or nothing at all
Whichever the gods decide.

BETTER OFF AS AIR

Nana Meta doesn't want to watch my 4th grade play,
even though I was the star.

I know this means she's dying.

I eat my imaginary cheeseburger
outside her hospital room because
my parents won't take me down to the cafeteria
and I'm hungry.

A couple years earlier
I find her lying on the kitchen floor
after a big thud wakes me out of bed.

I have never seen someone so clearly
as when I see her, flat on her back,
still holding a spoon.

She tells me that she's okay.

I can see that she is not okay.

I learn right then that hiding is what we do
for the people we love.

I suddenly feel like a giant.
I feel like my body is too big
and my voice is too loud
and I talk too much.

I apologize for my existence:
I'm sorry that I'm here.
I'm sorry about the way my stomach grumbles
when I'm hungry and the way my body

makes an indent in the chair and the way my breath
sounds in the silence.

Everyone seems to be running from something.
I join the race to get away.

I can't stop because someone might
trip over me, might find themselves
on the kitchen floor
getting trampled by all the things
they didn't want to see,
by the fact that they exist,
and the simple sadness of the way
our bodies refuse to merge,
no matter how tightly we hold on to each other.

 "We're not here," we whisper to ourselves as we run,
trampling the ones whose arms have gotten tired
of holding the world away,
and we don't dare stop to look or say we're sorry.

We don't want to end up on the kitchen floor,
admitting that we're not okay.

But what we can't see
as we close our eyes
and hold our breath
and run,
is the way

the ones on the floor are laughing,
the world collapsing in on them, shrieking
in the pain and joy of breathing, grateful
to have finally opened their eyes and seen
the face of God.

CIRCUS ANIMALS ARE BORING
7-22-99

First Oreos rule. Theres no doubt about it. Circus animals are boring. The least they could do is look like animals. The only weigh thats fun to eat Circus "blobs" is to bite there head off, but sometimes you can't even find it's head.

Next Oreo's frosting changes for the different Seasons or holidays. Red for Christmas, blue for Easter, and orange for Halloween! Circus animals are boring! There pink or white with sprinkles all the time and the taste. Ugh! it's grose!

Finally Oreos feel rough and look the coolest. I can't decide if the desighns are Greek or Egyptian, or an American who knew what kids would like. Circus animals are like the 15 hundreds coming back to haunt us. Oreos are like the year 2000 here already. Yeah, So Oreos around but the taste is what matters and they taste good. If I haven't said it yet, Oreos Rule!!!

AT ANY MOMENT, GOODBYE

I wonder how many times I have come here
Living through my body for years
Ignoring it and pretending pleasure
Is a trick of the Devil

And now I am captivated by a vein in my wrist
So delicate and vulnerable, moving as I write
Protected only by a thin, soft layer of skin

There is no way to know if he likes me
Or for how long
At any moment, goodbye
And yet suddenly
I am compelled to love fiercely regardless
With no thought of tomorrow or even
What will come next, not a hope
For a nuzzle and a kiss
Nor a fear of hiding eyes
Just the way the flowers on the sidewalk
make me want to dance
And painting my nails pink if I want to
Announcing:

Hello! Here I am!
I know you've been waiting for me too!

THE ALLEGORY OF THE PICNIC

It's as if everyone is pushing against the walls of a building, convinced that if they let go, the building will crumble.
"Look at you," they say to those lounging in the grass, enjoying a picnic, drawing the shapes they see in the clouds. "How can you afford to sit there idly, contributing nothing, playing Frisbee while the rest of us hold this building up?"

"Come play with us," the others reply, mouths full of sandwiches and wine.

"I couldn't leave this burden to the others," they say, the muscles in their arms starting to cramp.

"Suit yourself," say the ones in the grass, laughing and laying on each other's full bellies.

And perhaps out of guilt or a true fear, some never let go of that wall, keep holding it up, as if out of duty or penance or disbelief that they could deserve such a beautiful building, such a beautiful world, and be asked nothing in return.

So if you find yourself in a state of fatigue,
Remember this:

Let your arms rest.
The walls are strong enough to hold themselves.
You are not a pillar.
Your feet were made for dancing,
your hands for holding other hands,
for picking flowers.

THE WAY THE WORLD MELTS

I am sitting in my car, waiting
For Annie to come home
And invite me inside
So we can watch TV and order takeout
And I can tell her about
The boy I want
To kiss.

"He has a mustache," I'll tell her,
Even though it's not important,
Because I can't put into words
The way he looks familiar, like
Someone I didn't know I was
Missing, and the way my heart speeds up
And slows down at the same time
When he looks at me,
The way the world melts and I can finally
Relax.

I turned on the light so I could see the page,
Even though I prefer to sit here in the dark,
Watching the cars drive past me on the wet streets,
My head resting on the window,
Invisible and free.

PLACES I NEVER LIVED: THE HOUSE ON HARPER

My dad lived on Harper St. with my stepmom and stepsister during my late elementary school years. I never lived here, but I visited every other weekend and I had a turtle named Planéte who lived in the tiny pond in the front of the house. Leah, my stepsister, had a turtle named Rainbow Sparkle Princess or something like that.

All the rooms were painted different colors. Not boring colors like beige or white. They were red and blue and yellow and green. I don't remember if my room had a color, but I remember that it had round walls. I had never slept in a circle-shaped room before that. I didn't even know they existed.

CHAPTER THREE

Sometimes I feel so awkward I want to cut off my head and hand it to someone.

"Here," I'll say. "Just take it."

THE LOWER EAST SIDE

I remember, so vividly
Walking through the Lower East Side
Popping Advil like candy

I remember sitting at the bar
With a bottle of Pacifico
It was a Thursday

I remember the words
Some of us have to get up in the morning
I remember asking him to stay

I remember, so vividly
Waking up in the morning
Confused, and slightly scared

I remember almost fainting in the bathroom

The emergency room
And feeling fine
And being told I would have to stay

And I remember the man who walked
Back and forth down the hallway
The life nowhere near his eyes

And Annie bringing me a package of Hanes bikinis
And the windows, so thick and impossible
To open, 1st Avenue bustling nine stories below

And the man who always won Scrabble
And threw Reese's Peanut Butter Cups across the floor
And the girl who said the pills were helping

But today I am in Los Angeles
And my hands are dry
And I have to get up in the morning.

UNTITLED, BUT COULD BE CALLED "I'M WORRIED ABOUT TRAFFIC"
3-25-99

If I could fly like a bird, I would want to be the only one because if everyone could fly their would be a traffic jam in the sky. The advantages of flying are, I could get away from my enemies and fire. If thier is a traffic jam, I can get out of the car and fly. It would also be fun to fly. The disadvantages of flying is if I bump into something and fall it would be a long way down and I could get badly hurt. Another disadvantage is flying would probably use up a lot of energy.

MEANING OF LIFE

Sometimes I think I came into this world just to learn
To love myself
To see beauty in a piece of wood
In a cigarette butt on the sidewalk
In the way a tissue folds so elegantly
Emerged and waiting from its box.

It is easy to get caught in illusions—
The space between our bodies
The boy with the sparkly eyes
And the way he laughs and pays attention

So easy to believe that someone else
Could love you or not

The wood or tile floors
The placement of the windows in the bathroom
The way mom's face turned red
And livid, eyes round and
Popping, the love drained or hidden
In her grief

And now it's just me in my studio apartment
Reading books and wondering if I'll ever really feel
Like I belong

But still, there's something about the boy
With the sparkly eyes that makes me think
 Maybe I'm meant to be here after all

But what if his eyes lose their fire
Or his stars lead him away from mine
Will I then be left alone again, wondering
Where did I go?

———

A MIDNIGHT MIRACLE

I got out of bed and turned on the light
so that I could write down the poems
that were spilling into my thoughts,
running through in a decidedly male, British accent,
not unlike the voice of David Whyte.

And I can't help but wonder
at the ease in which I found
a notebook and a pen
just sitting atop a table at the foot of my bed
among the clutter, almost glowing,
as though someone had left them there for me,
knowing I would need them.

DIRECTIONS MY DAD GAVE ME ON THE PHONE

Drive down Sepulveda until you see Washington. Turn left on Washington. You'll see a taco restaurant on your left. It will be very busy. There's another one down the block and it will be empty. Don't stop, unless you're hungry. Keep driving and you'll pass Lincoln. There will be a lot of construction. You'll see Palawan only goes left. Pass it and make a U-turn and then turn right on Palawan. I'm going to take a shower. If you can take another wrong turn, it'll give me more time to get ready.

THE SYMPHONY

All I want to do is rock
back and forth under the tree tops
dangling like a firefly in the night,
bright as stars and alive enough
to eat.
I am not a soldier here.
I did not come to fight
against the death of our planet
and the way our skin
starts looking like rice paper
and the way our memories fade
into fiction.
I came to be present
in all of my discomfort
and joy,
to melt into the scenery
the way ice joins a steaming
cup of tea.
We are children,
awakening everyday
for the first time,
remembering only for convenience
our names.
Be who you are --
A single note in a symphony,
so beautiful and brave among the silence,
so eloquent and impossibly important.
Ephemeral, yet lasting in the way your body
moved space while you were here.
Find yourself in a new song.
Hear what you sound like beside another.
You are not alone.
You were not meant to be the whole song.

UNTITLED
2-19-99

When I grow up I will have dark brown hair down to a little below my
shoulders. I will have dark brown eye's. I probably would not wear make-
up very often. I will disine some of my own cloths. At fancy party's I will
wear a sparkly black dress with stalkings and sandle tipe highheels. For a
casual kind of dress I will wear a grey dress that is made out of this grey
sort of strechy matirial. It will be long sleeved and long. I will wear my hair
in a lot of diferent hair styles. I will be done with my braces so I will have
good teeth. I will sometimes wear jewlary but mostly earings. I will also
probably wear rings alot but not like Ms. Jill.

ALL THE GREAT POEMS

All the great poems have already been written
The ones that keep expanding
Every time you read them
Growing deeper and more true
Layered and flavorful, like wine
Containing, perhaps, more than even the writer
Had intended
Poems that grow as the world grows
So why should I continue to write
I have nothing to add to the conversation
Perhaps I should pack my bags and
Head home
Sit in my bed with a cup of tea and a movie
Or maybe just rest my head and get some sleep
And let my dreams
Take it from here

Food is my friend

Food is my friend

Food is my friend

Food is my friend

Food is my friend

Food is my friend

Food is my friend

Food is my friend

Food is my friend

Food is my friend

Food is my friend

Food is my friend

Food is my friend

Food is my friend

Food is my

friend

FRENCH TOAST AND BERRIES

The French Toast and berries are still on my mind
Partly because the dishes are still in my sink
But mostly because I wished for you my whole life
And the French Toast and berries are proof that you're
Real. I'm still not sure if I'm doing this right.
I can feel myself wanting to melt into you, all the way
Until our bodies don't make sense anymore,
Too small and solid for a love as big and bright
As ours.
Your hands are bigger than mine
And I like the way they look on my body,
Swallowing my stomach, my hips, my legs
I like it when you kiss me on my lips
Or anywhere. I'm afraid of the way you could
Disappear, my body left awake and wanting,
The space between our skin so dense and cold.
I don't know if I'm brave enough to melt
But I think I love you,
Even if part of me still wants to run and make
Excuses not to swallow and be swallowed.

A MOST PECULIAR SPOT

I find myself perched in a peculiar spot
A stop along my journey
Not even two blocks from my house
Not particularly pretty or picturesque
A spot upon a wall
Overlooking the hustle of traffic on a busy road
But today it sounds almost like ocean waves
And the people walking by me
Perhaps wonder to themselves
How I chose this most peculiar spot
To sit and write poetry
Rather than a coffee shop, say,
Or my kitchen table
Or a park with a fountain and a bench
And I think to that time in Maine
When after just a few psychedelic mushrooms
I looked around at the many rocks on the beach
Some of them occupied by sitting friends
And thought to myself
So desperately and in such despair
"I don't know where to sit!"
So now I implore you -- celebrate with me!
See me sitting here, with no quarrel or question
And look how far I've come!

A LOVE LIKE OURS

Even from across the country
We are living parallel lives
Taking acting classes
And improv
And splashing around
In matters of spirituality and the heart,
As they say.
Who would have thought
Either of us would end up here
So unexpected and seemingly random
To me, at least, despite childhood dreams
It's no wonder we met
But I still awe at the luck
That two peas like us could have found
A love like ours
We might not be sharing a pod anymore
But you're still my soulmate of soulmates
And I hope that one day soon
I wake up to you in the next room
And one of us jumps on the other
And we make breakfast
And cry from laughing

WE DIDN'T MAKE IT THROUGH THE WINTER

We didn't make it through the winter.

Even before the groundhog saw its shadow,
we stopped loving each other
and became afraid instead.
First me, then you quick to follow.

Worried about love
and whether or not we'd found it
instead of making it ourselves.

You are so crafty with your hands
but maybe your heart
hasn't had as much practice.
And I am a wanderer
and not yet sure of why I'm here
or what love even looks like.

Maybe it's too early to be writing a poem.

After all,
the embers are still hot and glowing
and perhaps all it would take
is some crumpled newspaper
and a wooden log.

It seems so final on the page.

But maybe
we're just ready to go home
tired of the company
and aching for our beds.

—

I'm eating raw cookie dough
with a spoon as I write this,
which tells you something: that

I miss the fire and fear the cold.

But I don't know where you are
or what you're thinking
or if God has other plans for me
or if I get to make the plans this time.

I'd crumple the newspaper
and throw it in, just so you know,
even without a log,
just for another flame or two.

I'm cold, but not yet tired
and if I were to go to bed
I'd spend all night awake
and thinking.

WHAT EVEN IS A REAL JOB

Being a poet doesn't seem like a real job
Not like a painter
Who uses so much skill
The imitation of shadows,
The mixing of color,
The use of imagination and great attention
To detail

Not like a novelist, who builds whole worlds
Gives birth to characters who seem more real sometimes
Than my own adolescence

Or even a politician, with knowledge
And agenda

A poem seems so small and often quite
Incomplete
A job anyone can do
If they know how to listen
And perhaps
That is the true value of a poet after all,
Not as a writer,
But as one who can hear the buzzing
In her ears, who can hear the Great Universe
And all the things it has to say,
Mostly, "You're beautiful"
          "I love you"
          "You are worthy of your voice"

PLACES I NEVER LIVED: CHRYSTIE

The Chrystie St. apartment was located in Chinatown in New York City. I always felt at home there, though often also out of place. There were two couches in the living room, a feat that was always, in my opinion, worthy of jealousy and conversation, especially when hunting for an apartment myself. They were very comfortable to sleep on and I slept on them any chance I could get.

I don't have a lot of specific memories from this apartment, even though I was there a lot. Maybe we listened to music and talked. I probably watched people smoke weed. Maybe we drank beer. Once, I definitely remember, we made a pie.

A few years after I moved to Los Angeles, I visited the boys in their new apartment in Bushwick. They had brought only one of the couches with them and of course, this is where I slept. I noticed that the color was faded, and the cushions seemed lumpier.

CHAPTER FOUR

I hate leaving karaoke night wondering, "Did I choose the right song?"

ADVICE FROM THE FLOOR OF MY BEDROOM, REVISED

Try to have as many fun experiences as you can when you're young.

They might be the only things that give you hope later when you get older and nothing is going your way.

YOU SHOULD NEVER SMOKE. ONCE YOU START, IT'S HARD TO STOP
7-15-99

First you can get cancer and die from smoking! The smoke goes into your lungs, then you realize you have cancer. The next thing you know, you'll see your friends and family at your funeral.

Next it's not good for the people around you. What if you were walking near an old person, they can't take the smoke. Next thing you know they're in the hospital. Think about other people as well as yourself.

Finally, there are little red beetles in cigarettes. That's gross! Who would want to smoke beetles?! If you do, you need to go to a mental hospital.

So if you want to smoke beetles, be inconsiderate to others, and die from cancer, smoke. If you don't, take my advice, don't smoke.

HERMIT CRABS

Yesterday I discovered hermit crabs
And I wonder if they are aesthetically inclined
Or if they have no idea how beautiful their shells are
Maybe they were just looking for something that fits
And when I think about them, it makes me cry for some reason
Maybe because a tide pool is so simple
And unassuming
So responsive to the touch
Even to a ripple in the water
Maybe it's just such a surprise and delight
To see a pretty shell get up
And take a stroll.

THE BODY

I have tried to be good
And right
And worthy of compliments
And friendship

But a girl can't live
Without magic
And romance
And music

The lights of the Ferris wheel on the pier
Flash as if to say
"You've made it"

The music
Tickles
And simmers the blood

And all this time
I thought it was a boy
Or a job
Or a thing of the past

Too many nights inside
When the stars are twinkling
Against a black and endless sky

Too many days
Following the same route
To the coffee shop

The magic in the palm trees
In the pink clouds
In the cold sand

In the music
So desperate to embody, to caress
The ears
The bones
The blood

The body, I'm learning
Was not made to lead the band
The body was made to dance along
To sing
To skip
To wander

I DON'T HAVE MUCH TO SAY ABOUT IT

The grass is green.
I don't have much to say about it.
And of course, the sky is blue.
And my pen is black and bored.

ADVENTURE

I used to think adventure was a road trip with a full car
To places I'd never been
A long journey around the world
To meet new and unexpected people
To have my heart broken open
And to come home with a story

Maybe there are margaritas
Or cartwheels in the street
And laughing until our stomachs hurt

But is there room for lows?
The breakdowns
And the long stretches with nothing to do
And is there room for silence
And ordinary conversation?

I always think I have to go somewhere far away
Meet someone new
Kiss a stranger
Run through the hills and
Scream from the tops of mountains

But maybe an adventure could be
Just getting up from your chair because you want to
Using the bathroom
Walking up and down the hall
A sapling of a poem tiptoeing across your brain
And then finding, luckily, a pad of paper and a pen
And writing it all down.

THE IMPROV JAM

Name
Bucket
Sit
Wait
Drink
Laugh
Cole
Morgan
Bucket
Heartbeat
Name
Name
Name
Sit
Laugh
Cringe
Laugh
Clap
Repeat
Repeat
Repeat
Cole
Morgan
Bucket
Name
Stage
Heartbeat
Talk
Move
Talk
Move
Sit
Drink
Laugh

Clap

Laugh

Clap

Cringe

Laugh

Clap

Repeat

Morgan

Cole

Montage

Montage

(Montage)

Drink

Home

Sleep

UNTITLED, BUT COULD BE CALLED "PUDDING"
4-16-99

The food that I don't want to live without is pudding. Well, not all pudding. Just homemade pudding. Pudding is my favorite dessert. My favorite flavors go in this order, Butterscotch, vanella, then chocolate. One of the reasons I like pudding is because you don't have to chew it. When I was younger I loved pudding so much that when I was done, I would have my mom or dad get me the rest of the pudding that might be left on the sides of the container or bowl. Also when I was younger I used to love eating pudding with the realy realy small spoon because it was fun and it took longer to eat.

FIRE

I wish I could settle for kindness
And shoulder kisses in the morning
And French toast
But as it is, I want fire
I want to feel like time has stalled
To let us enjoy ourselves just a little bit longer
Than science would allow
Maybe I'm a fool
But it seems worth it for 3am
Awake with you, alone
With fire in our eyes
Between our legs
Saying, whatever this is, I like it

I'M BETTER AT SLEEPING

I'm afraid
That who I am
Will never be heard

Who am I?

I know who I
Try to be:
Perfect

Creative
Funny
Capable

I don't do a very good job
I'm better at sleeping

I know I like:
Coffee shops
And Christmas time

I liked fireflies
The few times I saw them.
Other than that

I can't think of much
Just purple mountains
And sunset clouds

And the bigness
Of the ocean
And the moon

But those are just

—

Decorations
Gifts from the universe

Nothing I made
Or know what to do with.

PLACES I NEVER LIVED: CROSBY

The apartment on Crosby St. was at the top of 6 flights of stairs. I would always have to stop to catch my breath before I knocked on the door. The floor of the living room was slanted, which was perfect for making brass monkeys. A brass monkey is a 40 oz Colt 45 mixed with orange juice. You can't mix it by shaking, because it's carbonated, so you have to roll it. The slanted floor seemed to be made for this purpose.

Each room in the apartment was painted a different color. I helped paint them, which was a fact that always gave me a sense of purpose and belonging.

One time we took mushrooms and stayed up all night. We made a mess. I think a chair broke. Someone fainted in the bathtub. If you were to ask us about it, we'd say we were just trying to go horizontal. Horizontal, we thought, was the natural position of things. When I started to come down, the slanted floor and messy living room gave me anxiety, so I left and walked home at 5am. I remember thinking the city was very vertical, and that no one on mushrooms would ever build such a vertical city.

CHAPTER FIVE

New York is like that passionate romance that can't last
because he'll never love you the way you want him to
and also he smells like pee.

HEAVY WITH WATER AND MUSIC

The night was warm and the mosquitoes wanted blood
And we, of course, we wanted love

But we couldn't say it

So we danced and the air was hot
And heavy with water and music

When the rain finally showed itself
I saw you in all your terrifying beauty
So straight on your feet
Strong, and your hair was wild

I don't know what you saw in me
Intoxicated with ecstasy and booze
I wanted to say: *You turn my blood electric*
I like it when you touch me

But I couldn't say it

So we danced and the air was hot
And heavy with water and music

And the night was warm
And the mosquitoes wanted blood

LIGHT REFLECTING OFF OF THINGS

Sometimes, when it's raining
Or when I catch the sunset
In my rearview mirror
Or when I close my eyes
While I brush my teeth
Or when the birds fly over houses
Laughing at the way that I worry
About whether or not

I'm loved

I suddenly remember that I'm dancing
In a House of Mirrors, that
All I am is light
Reflecting off of things.
And in those moments
I wish I could eat my surroundings.
I wish I could consume the whole world and feel
Full.

AND YOU LIKE IT

The thing about morality is
It works until
The thing you protested,
Said you would never do
Crawls up your skirt and tickles you
And you like it
And then you have to decide
If it's worth it to punish and condemn
Or if perhaps you prefer, after all,
A world without so many rules.

But how, you might ask,
Are you then supposed to know
What's right and how to be good?

Well, it might be messy
And not what you had hoped for
But in the end, you'll know
Who you really are
And you'll be able to live in each moment
Without a preconceived no
Or a pressured yes
And you might say

I don't know any of the answers

And then you might laugh
Or cry
Or hear something you've never heard before
And finally you'll know what it means to be
Alive.

FRENEMIES

QWERTYUIOP
 ASDFGHJKL
 ZXCVBNM

I WONDER

I'm most creative at
Night
Or with a glass of wine
Getting in the way of my
Judgment

And I wonder if that's cheating
On the road to success

And I wonder why
So many rules
And I wonder when
I will feel free to be myself
And I wonder how
Many
Kinks
In my
Neck
Until
I get
Comfortable.

And I wonder and I wonder
And I wonder
And it is a rare day that I take
An action
Write a poem
Or bake a pie
It is a rare day
That I do something
Other than sleep
And eat
And wonder.

THE PROCESS OF BECOMING ENLIGHTENED

yes no yes no yes no no yes no yes yes yes no yes no yes no no no no
yes no yes no yes yes yes no no yes no yes no no no yes no no no no no
yes yes no yes yes yes yes yes yes no yes no yes yes yes yes no yes no
no no yes yes yes yes yes no yes yes no yes no yes yes yes yes yes
no no yes no yes no no no no yes yes no yes no yes no yes yes yes yes
yes yes yes yes yes no yes yes yes yes no yes no yes yes no yes no no no
yes no no yes no yes no yes no yes yes no no no no yes no yes no yes
yes yes no no yes no yes no yes no yes no yes yes no no yes no yes no
yes no yes no yes no no no no yes yes yes yes no yes no yes yes yes no
no no yes yes no yes no yes no yes no yes no yes no yes no no no yes
yes yes no yes no yes no yes yes yes yes yes yes no yes yes yes no no
yes yes no yes no yes no yes yes yes no no yes yes no yes no yes no yes
no yes no yes no no no yes no yes no no no no no no no no no yes no no
no no yes no yes no yes no yes no yes no yes no yes no yes no yes no no
yes yes no yes no yes no yes no yes yes yes no no yes no yes no yes no
yes yes no yes no no yes no yes no yes no yes no yes yes yes no no yes
yes yes no yes no yes no yes no yes yes no no yes no yes no yes no no
yes no yes yes no yes yes no no yes no yes no yes no yes no yes no yes
yes yes no no yes no yes no yes no no yes no yes no yes yes no no no
yes yes no yes no yes no yes no yes no yes no no yes no yes yes no yes
no yes yes no no yes no yes no yes no yes no no no no yes yes no yes no yes
yes yes yes yes yes no yes no yes yes no yes no yes yes yes no yes no no
no yes no yes no yes no yes no yes yes yes no yes yes yes no yes no yes
no yes yes no no no no yes no yes no yes no no yes yes yes yes no yes
yes yes

BUTTERFLY WISHES

What does a butterfly do
After it's landed on flowers
Time and time again,
After it's flown over green fields
In the valleys of mountains
And seen the sun again?

Does it feel bored?
Does it wish to be,
After all its efforts of becoming,
A part of the earth again?

YOU ARE SO UTTERLY DIVINE

You are so utterly Divine.
You are so
Magnificently
Radiantly
Beautifully
Magically
Brilliantly
Splendidly
Wonderfully
Preciously
Exquisitely
Perfectly
Almost lazily
Divine.

LAND

I am beginning to see the world
For just a moment here and there, just a glimpse
Through the eyes of someone whose house was never bulldozed
Or burned
Or maybe it was more like a subtle tearing,
An unraveling at the seams until you find your world
Turned to thread
Nothing to comfort and cozy

And of course, with all that string
Who wouldn't try to make something beautiful
But maybe just for a moment

I guess what I'm trying to say is
I never knew a stable life
And have become so used to living on the boat
Maybe what I'm glimpsing is land
Could it be?
After so much time, could I really build a house again?
And could I really live there?

THE COUCH

So comfy.
Never leave.

SCIENCE IS INVOLVED

I don't think I have the "fix it" gene.
I'll give you an example:

I carry a good 20 pounds
of unnecessary weight on my body
And have for some time,
But rarely do I work out,
And rarely do I see a chocolate chip cookie
Or a blueberry scone and think,
Better not.

As I watch the farmer's market pack up,
Closing their tents,
It occurs to me for a moment
That science is involved—
The system of elbows
That enables those tents to open and close
So simply,
And I notice that I don't have a need,
That there's beauty in a dirty fork
And I have no impulse to wash it.
I'm rarely curious, sometimes inquisitive,
Mostly observant,
Admiring, thinking…

I think you can tell a lot about a person
By finding out what they would do
If left in a room all by themselves.

Some, I imagine, would try to get out,
Plan their escape,
Look for cracks and openings.

Some might find something to draw with,

—

Make lists on the walls
Or draw landscapes
Or faces.

I think I would just sit there and ponder,
Probably take a nap,
Stare at the ceiling and think,
Notice the way white
looks different with a shadow on it.

LOVE TIMES TWO

Love
Times Two

Me
Plus You
Plus Another

A bed
A table
A dinner
A neighbor

Me
Plus You
Plus Love
Times Two

Don't drink
After midnight

Don't walk
Across the street
Without shoes

Don't lounge
And sip
And show
Your legs

Don't laugh
And scream
And drink
After midnight

Love
Times two

Me
Plus you
Plus Another

Wet
And cozy
And drunk
With a sputter

Me
Plus You
Plus Love
Plus another.

23 STEPS TO FINDING YOUR SOUL:

Step 1: Declare that you want to find your soul.

Step 2. Stop wearing makeup and straightening your hair.

Step 3. Go about your days, doing as you do. Be super happy sometimes. Be super depressed sometimes.

Step 4. Become curious about the Universe in a big way. Realize nothing is as it seems. (Do psychedelics for the first time).

Step 5. Experience a tragedy or devastation of some kind. A familial death, life-threatening injury, divorce, or trying to kill yourself with Advil and alcohol will do.

Step 6. Seek out and/or stumble upon something having to do with spiritual awakening. Read about it and/or take a class about it.

Step 7. Fall completely under the spell of whatever it was you stumbled upon having to do with spiritual awakening. Give that person, organization, book, or idea your full faith and attention.

Step 8. Forget who you are completely while under the guise of "finding yourself."

Step 9: Feel terrible a lot.

Step 10. Realize you fell into a trap.

Step 11. Resent the person, organization, book, or idea that trapped you.

Step 12: Judge yourself for falling into the trap and giving yourself up to something outside of yourself.

Step 13. Re-learn to trust yourself.

—

Step 14: Forgive the person, organization, book, or idea that trapped you. You realize it's not their fault and that you actually learned a lot from them.

Step 15: Vow to take dominion over your own life.

Step 16: Start wearing makeup again because you want to look pretty for the boy you like.

Step 17: Wonder if you've even learned anything.

Step 18: Continue learning to trust yourself.

Step 19: Take a risk.

Step 20: Feel what it feels like to trust yourself and realize the Universe totally supports you.

Step 21: Repeat Step 18.

Step 22: Never find your soul, because you discover that you are your soul. Become more soul-like.

Step 23: Feel that the word "soul" is void of meaning and decide to stop using it altogether.

THIS COULD BE PARADISE

This could be paradise
The sky rarely turning a shade
Other than blue or pink
Or black
The ocean sparkling
Like a glass of Prosecco
And the nights!
Can you think of anything more romantic
Than a bicycle and a breeze
That only barely kisses the leaves
And nothing but a whirring in the ears
Like a whisper
The silence so ticklish and inviting
The neighborhood alive in its quiet darkness
Houses and trees and empty roads
A light here and there
Santa Monica, I never knew
That you could be so romantic
Palm trees like long, bare legs
Flowers like a first date

—

AN ADMISSION OF INNOCENCE

And finally I surrender
A blank flag waving faintly in the breeze
Awaiting instruction
An admission of innocence
And ignorance
And if I were to close my eyes
It wouldn't make much difference
I am not seeing clearly
My conclusions are outdated
And often simply wrong
And as the bigger picture comes into view
Larger and more detailed and quite unexpected
I have no choice but to wait for it
And delight in it
And choose accordingly

UNTITLED
10-2-98

When I grow up I want to be a hair dresser, an inventer, or a writter. I love
doing peoples hair. My favoret is styaling, but I also like cutting hair. I love
scianse and inventing. I love making gak and slime. I love trying to figur
out how to make difrent things like robots. I love writting also. I want to
write diffrent childrens books. I want to invent a time machine or wright a
book called, A Cat In A Dogs Position #2 (My cousin is writting #1.) Or if I
have enouf time I will do all of them.

PLACES I NEVER LIVED: E. 7th ST.

I almost lived in the apartment on E. 7th St, but for some reason my roommates and I decided to move to Brooklyn instead. I think we were trying to be adventurous. We moved into a building nicknamed The Rocket Factory in Williamsburg. Our apartment had a giant kitchen and a living room that could have easily fit two couches, but had barely any bedrooms. My bedroom, for example, might have been considered the top bunk to Emily's room. You had to climb a ladder to get in. I planned to live in there with Brittany because we didn't want to spend too much money on rent or too much time away from each other.

When we moved our stuff in, the apartment was trashed. There was a broken bed frame in the middle of the floor. There were dishes still in the dishwasher. There were empty whip-it canisters in the kitchen drawers and I'm pretty sure there was a needle somewhere lying about, though my traumatized mind might have added that part. But there was definitely egg yolk, all over everything. A few days after we moved in, we were attacked by bed bugs. And then the electricity went out and then I lost my voice. We only lived there for a month, and we mostly slept elsewhere. I spent a few nights in the NYU library. If you pushed two chairs together, it felt like you were lying in a crib.

I remember sitting with Emily at our favorite café, desperately wondering if this was what adult life was like, just stress and anxiety and trying to solve complex problems like how to get out of our yearlong lease after only a week. A man who looked to be in his 40s was sitting next to us with a giant chocolate chip cookie on his plate. I think we both secretly hoped he would turn to us, comfort us, tell us that no, what we were going through sounded unusual. But he didn't turn to us, and we continued to wonder.

Meanwhile, Jessica and her roommates moved into the apartment on E 7th St. One of her roommates was a dog named Jagger and I remember holding him while dancing to Iggy Pop. Jessica lived there for a long time, longer than I had ever lived anywhere since high school. A few days before I moved to Los Angeles, I threw a going away party on the roof.

www.ingramcontent.com/pod-product-compliance
Lightning Source LLC
Chambersburg PA
CBHW051735040426
42447CB00008B/1145